THE
STORY
OF
NEW
YORK'S
STAIRCASE

THE STORY OF NEW YORK'S STAIRCASE

A Heatherwick Studio Design

PRESTEL
Munich · London · New York

CONTENTS

INTRODUCTION

7

UP, UP AND AWAY

DESIGNING AND MAKING
NEW YORK'S STAIRCASE

Jeff Chu

36

A WEST SIDE STORY

HUDSON YARDS,
THE NEW HEART OF NEW YORK

Sarah Medford

80

MOVEMENT AS MONUMENT

A TWENTY-FIRST-CENTURY
PUBLIC SPACE

Paul Goldberger

102

PICTURE CREDITS

140

AUTHOR BIOGRAPHIES

141

Introduction

From its earliest conception, Hudson Yards was a gathering place. The developers of this built-from-scratch neighborhood intended to bring people together in an entirely new way, to create a different kind of civic engagement and social interaction in a city already known to foster the best of both. So it is fitting that at the center of Hudson Yards—at the center of the new heart of New York—there should be a unique public landmark that stands out, a one-of-a-kind structure that only a visionary could imagine. Created as much to be climbed on as gazed upon, at once powerful and whimsical, profound and elemental, the interconnected staircases by Heatherwick Studio are meant to be a platform for every expression of life in this city for years to come. Indeed, every journey on these flights of fancy will be different from previous ones and from those that follow, each individual experience shared with the new multitudes who have gathered on and around it.

This is the story of that remarkable work.

A truly monumental welcome, an experience that brings people together.

INTENTION

We are all participants in a great movement. In every quadrant of the globe—in Shanghai and London, in Rio and Delhi, in Paris and Johannesburg—people are coming together in ever greater numbers to work, to live, to play. Half of humanity can be found in the world's great cities, with more flowing in daily. Some come for a few hours, some for a few weeks, some forever. But all seek the energy and connection that city life offers. Perhaps no city better represents such a unique combination of excitement and opportunity than New York. And seeing Hudson Yards as the new center of this most global of crossroads, its developers understood that they needed to offer a truly monumental welcome: a magnet for business, a North Star for dreamers, and an experience that literally brings people together, whether they have arrived from across the street or from across an ocean.

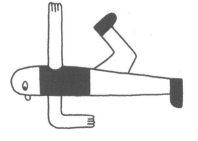

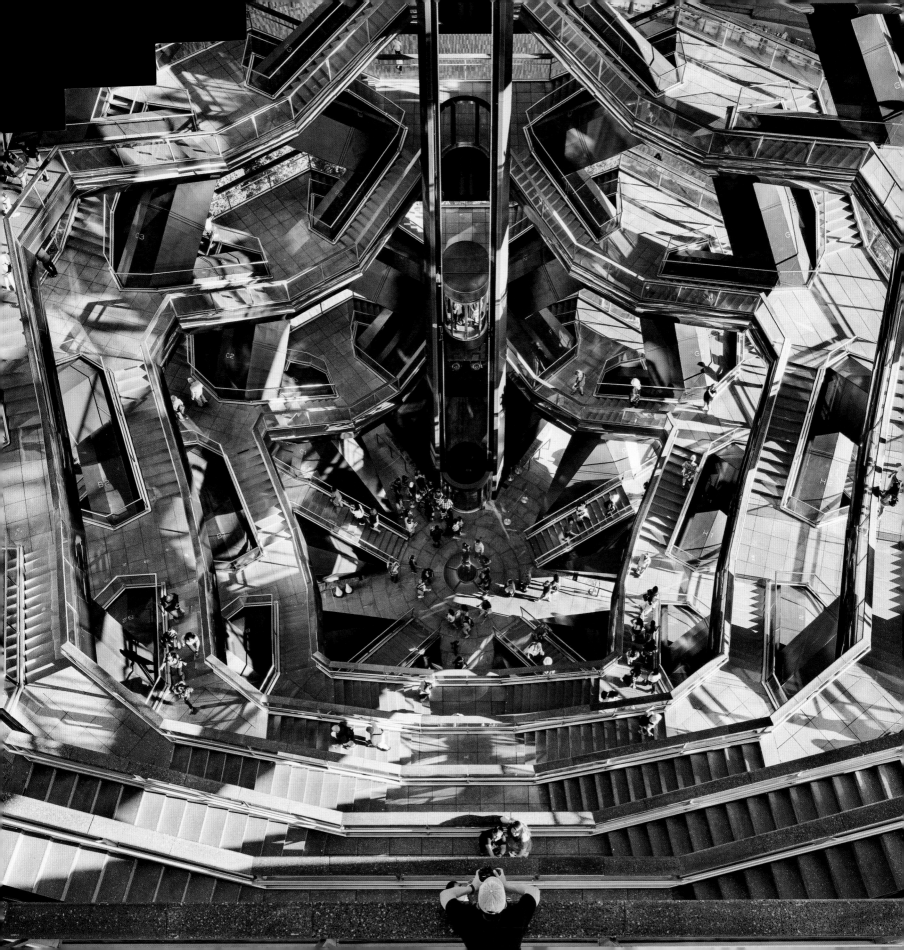

Something 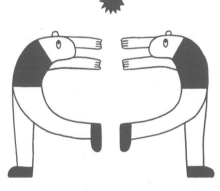 amazing that people

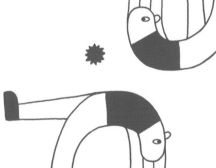

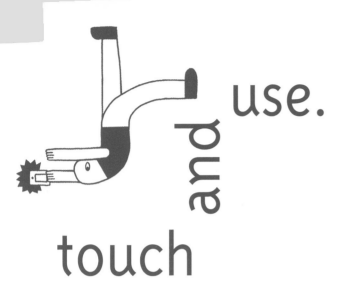

touch and use.

IDEATION

Creativity is indeterminate. Although Heatherwick Studio needed only a couple of months to devise the basic concept of the staircase—and Stephen Ross, developer of Hudson Yards, needed just one viewing to anoint it—the monument was millennia in the making. A far-reaching timeline of inspirations came to bear on its final design, including ancient stepwells in India, the work of artist M. C. Escher, a playground in London, and the High Line park that wraps around Hudson Yards. Only from such disparate wellsprings could Thomas Heatherwick and the studio team realize their simple but profound desire for "something amazing that people touch and use."

UP, UP AND AWAY

DESIGNING AND MAKING NEW YORK'S STAIRCASE

Jeff Chu

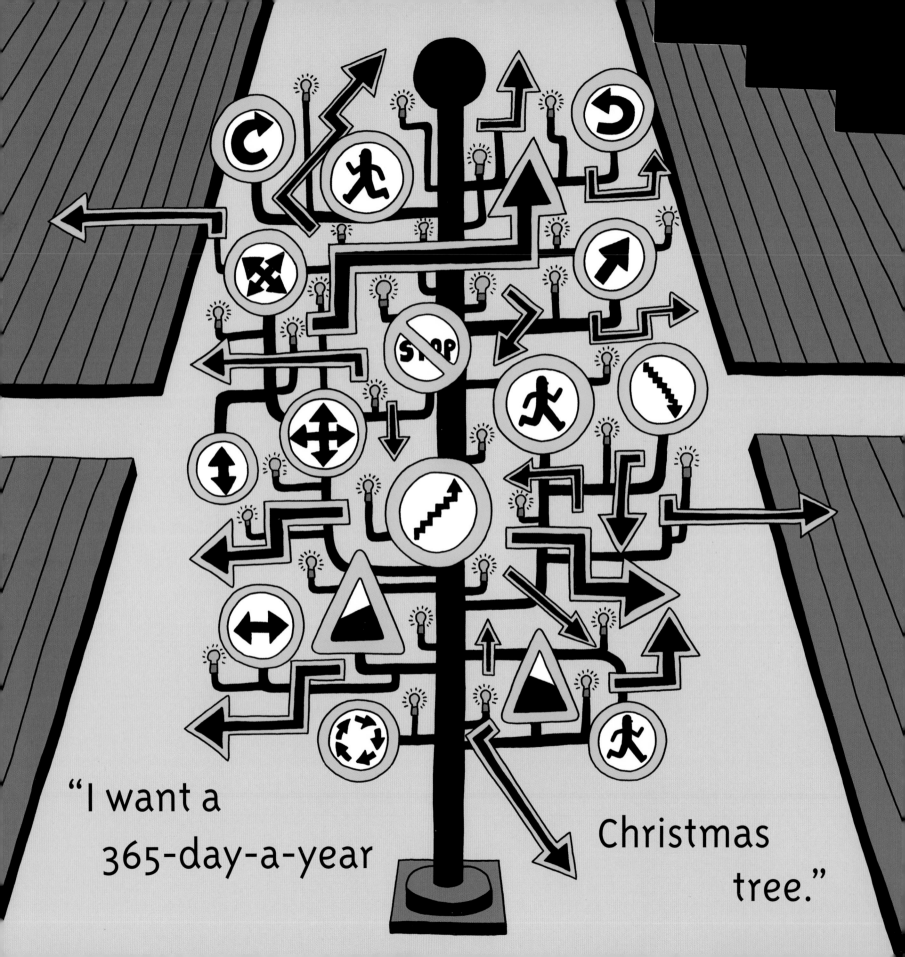

"It's a monument."
"It's a sculpture."
"It's half a pineapple."
"It's a staircase."

What is it? In the strictest terms, the dramatic centerpiece at Hudson Yards is a unique, mostly steel structure, the primary attention-grabber in New York City's newest neighborhood. What it is not is a building; it has no roof and no rooms. And although it has stairs—lots of stairs—don't be misled: the pinnacle is no more a destination than any other part of it.

"It's a giant woven basket."
"It's a puzzle."
"It's a beehive."

It can be, and is, all of these things. Which also makes the piece a kind of riddle, with no single correct answer. And that is by design. Thomas Heatherwick, who led the creative team that designed the staircase, says: "I love things that don't tell me what to think of them."

That said, a lot of thinking went into the formation of this hard-to-define structure, not least because of the challenge posed by the L-shaped space that hosts it. It fell first to the landscape architecture firm Nelson Byrd Woltz to tame this unorthodox footprint.

One inspiration was the Piazza del Campidoglio in Rome. In that unusual, trapezoidal space, Michelangelo used lighter paving stones against a background of dark ones to create an elegant oval and a network of interlaced arcs on the ground. Equally relevant, a statue of the emperor Marcus Aurelius serves as a focal point in this space with no obvious center.

For Hudson Yards, name partner Thomas Woltz and his team sketched out what he calls a "twenty-first-century meditative labyrinth of harmonic curves and forms." This network, also created with variably shaded materials, connects the entrances of the surrounding buildings with subtly elliptical and overlapping paths. "Any human body engaging the space is gently embraced into its center," Woltz explains. "It has a real centripetal force."

The original plan called for some sort of monumental object at the plaza center, a unifying force around which the rest of the landscape would evolve. That dovetailed with the long-held conviction of Stephen Ross—chairman of Related Companies, co-developer of the site with Oxford Properties—that public space must be more than an expanse of pavement. Public space needs an iconic feature to make it compelling. Rockefeller Center, for instance, has its Christmas tree. "I want a 365-day-a-year Christmas tree," Ross told friends and colleagues.

The metaphor telegraphed the ambitions for the anchoring object— not least of which was that it had to be more than a mere object. A Christmas tree, after all, offers not only visual spectacle but emotional resonance, stirring memories as it shines its light. At Rockefeller Center, it is also both destination and place-maker as well.

At Hudson Yards the object would have to be that and something more: a sign to everyone—and especially prospective commercial tenants—that the developers were serious about making good on their promises and timelines. This heavy burden was one of many reasons Ross was for a long time alone in his conviction that Hudson Yards would be incomplete without a spectacular attraction at its center. "Most people didn't understand what I wanted," Ross says. "The rest told me I was crazy."

For a while it looked like the doubters might be right, as the developer sat through one unconvincing presentation after another from some of the most creative minds in the world. Then, one day, Ross visited Storm King Art Center in Orange County, New York, hoping to draw inspiration from its famed open-air sculpture collection. A colleague on the two-hour drive brought along a copy of the

Opposite: The atrium at Zeitz Museum of Contemporary Art Africa in Cape Town, South Africa. The museum, designed by Heatherwick Studio, is carved out of concrete grain silos.

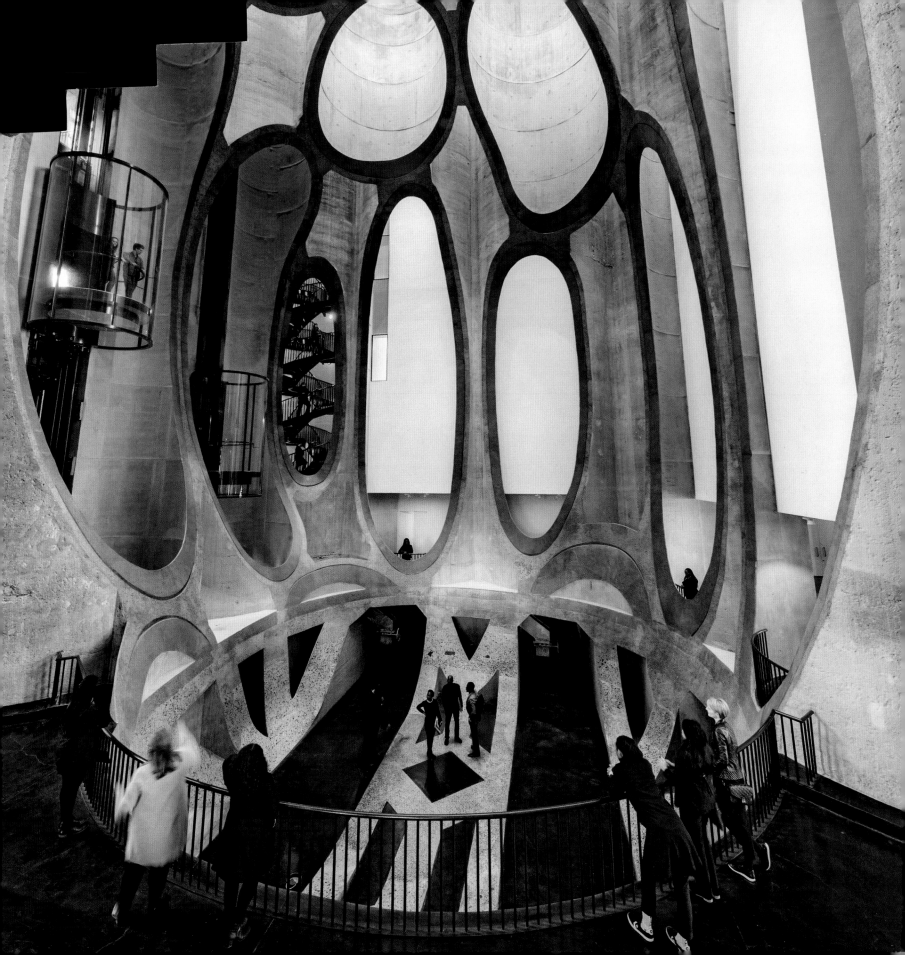

Practical Magic

Selected projects by Heatherwick Studio

Left: The Learning Hub, also known as The Hive, at Nanyang Technological University in Singapore was designed to foster classroom collaboration.

Below: The Rolling Bridge was completed in 2004 and installed at Paddington Basin in London.

Above: The New Routemaster, the first new London bus design in more than five decades, is a more time- and energy-efficient version of the classic double-decker.

Left: The cauldron for the 2012 Summer Olympics in London was composed of individual copper pieces carried into the stadium by representatives of each country.

book *Thomas Heatherwick: Making*. Heatherwick, founder of the London-based design practice Heatherwick Studio, was already renowned for such inspired work as London's Rolling Bridge, the 2012 Olympic cauldron, and the Seed Cathedral at 2010's Shanghai Expo.

Ross was intrigued. Soon after, he met with Heatherwick and his colleagues from the studio, both in New York and London, to discuss a "thing" that would both anchor a plaza and invite passersby to interact with it. As the studio team interpreted it, the request was for more than a physical object: it was for an engaging narrative. "It felt as if something would be more of a place-maker if people used it and touched it, rather than just looking at and admiring it and asking, 'Oh, what were they thinking when they made that?'" Heatherwick says.

Put another way, some creations force you to focus on the designer's thinking. Heatherwick wanted instead to elevate the imaginations and experiences of those who encounter it. "It seemed more generous to make something that didn't define itself as art," he says. "Is it mathematics? Is it Escher? You decide."

Early on, the solution to Related's brief took shape around stairs. "We talked about stairs at amazing length," says Laurence Dudeney, Heatherwick Studio's lead on the project. "Stairs create social spaces." Heatherwick himself has long been intrigued by stairs. In college, he once happened upon a discarded Victorian staircase—a full flight of sixteen steps—and maneuvered it onto the roof of his car to transport it to his studio. Later, he helped design a jungle gym for a primary school, part of which loomed over the entrance that parents passed through to pick up their kids. "Children love looking down on their mums and dads—the big adults beneath the small children; it's empowering," Heatherwick says. "But why are climbing frames for children only? Why can't they be for playful adults as well?"

Heatherwick Studio took one cue from ancient Rome. Its historic amphitheaters certainly succeeded in both place-making and people-gathering functions, and their concentric circular tiers offered an

Above: Early on, the Heatherwick Studio team marked out the stairs and landings to help them visualize user experience and circulation.

Opposite: The staircase will remind some of the work of M. C. Escher. One example: his 1953 lithograph *Relativity*.

Overleaf: Researching potential forms, the team explored amphitheaters and stepwells like Panna Meena ka Kund in the city of Amer in Rajasthan, India.

intriguing form. What vexed the design team, however, was the visual blandness of the exteriors. From the outside, an amphitheater is forbidding—a giant, nonporous bowl. Inside, light enters only from above. "You can't see out of it," Heatherwick says. "Our question was, how could you cut lots of holes in it so it's not impenetrable?"

The breakthrough came when a team member shared images of Indian stepwells. Most common in the northwestern Indian states of Gujarat and Rajasthan, these interconnected arrangements of stairs and landings were constructed hundreds of years ago to access the subterranean water table. But they soon became gathering places; in the punishing heat, it was cooler in these painstakingly hewn oases.

Of course, there was no way to build downward at Hudson Yards, which sits on a platform atop working rail yards. So Heatherwick Studio upended the stepwell concept, devising a stairs-and-landing framework that would ultimately rise 150 feet above the platform. Fifty feet in diameter at its base, it widens to 150 feet at the top.

And so it was that, only a couple of months after the first meetings with Ross, Thomas Heatherwick and studio group leader Stuart Wood flew to New York to present the idea for the staircase—including a model and slide presentation—to most of the Related senior team, which included CEO Jeff Blau, president Bruce Beal, COO Ken Wong, Related Hudson Yards president Jay Cross, and executive vice president Emad Lotfalla, who oversaw construction for the project. Ross's colleagues were skeptical, to say the least, concerned about everything from feasibility to cost. But Ross was a believer from the beginning. "I knew it when I saw it," he says. "That's what I wanted."

Right: This diagram sequence shows Heatherwick Studio's idea to raise the public square itself, creating a tiered, open space.

Opposite: During the concept-design stage, the team experimented with various amphitheater-like forms before devising the open lattice structure that was presented to the developers.

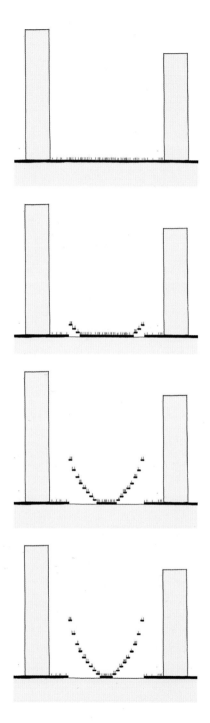

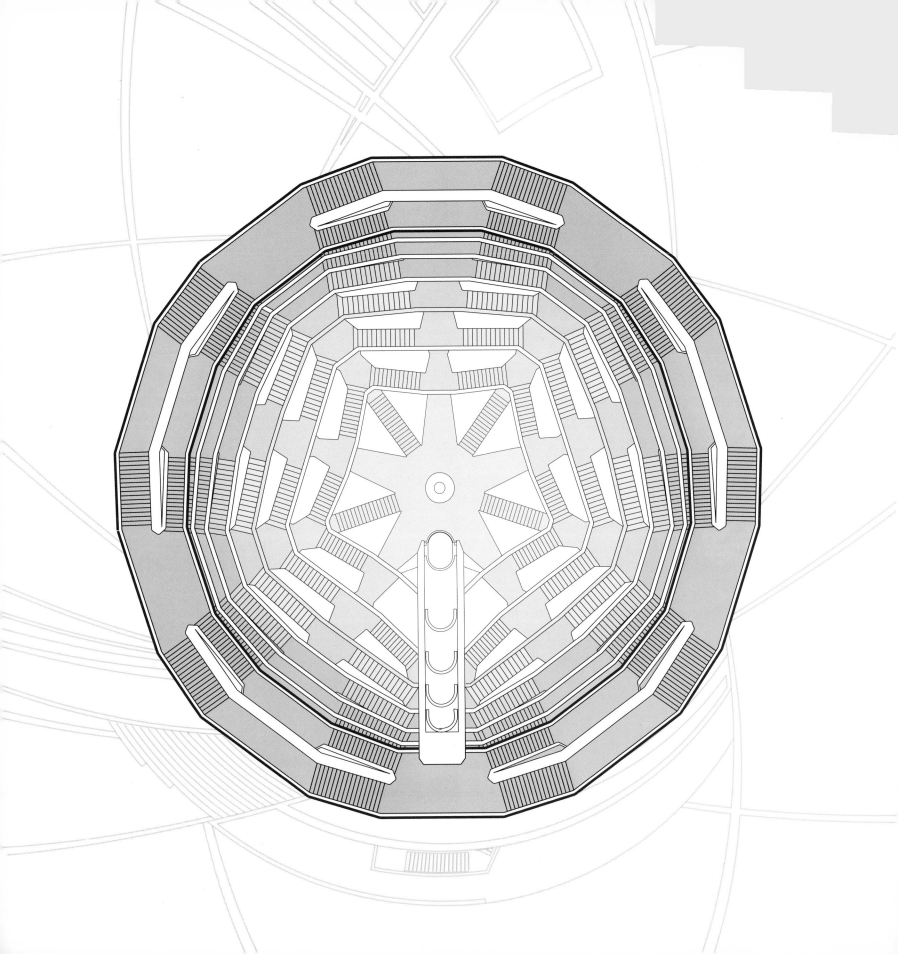

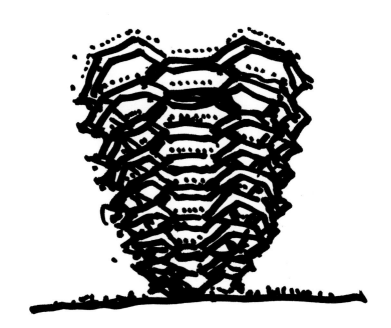

Above: An original Thomas Heatherwick
sketch of the staircase.

Opposite: A computer-produced schematic
of the staircase from above. The tunnel-like detail
at the bottom represents the elevator track.

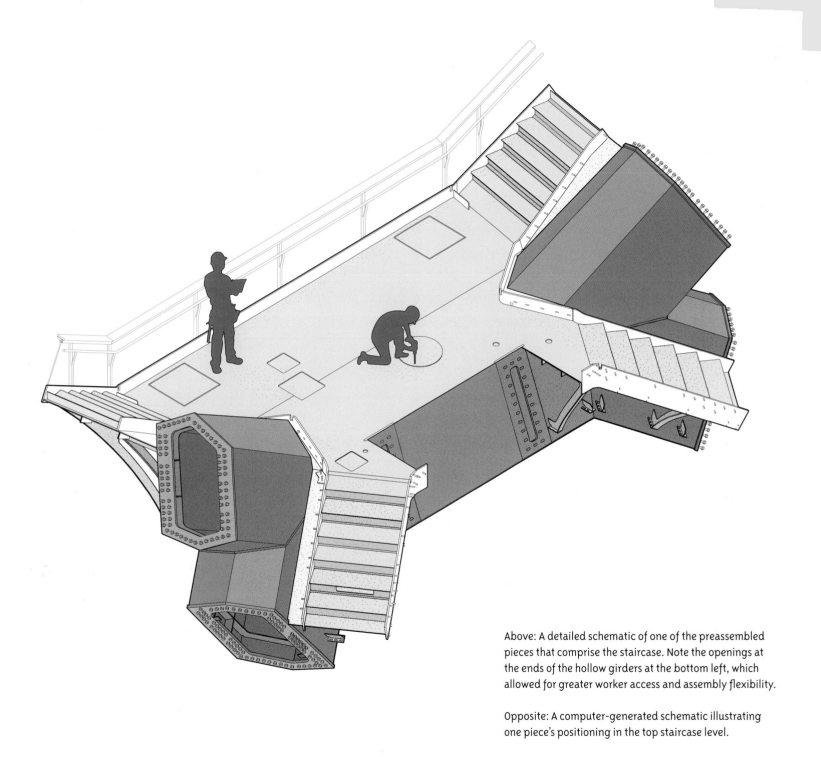

Above: A detailed schematic of one of the preassembled pieces that comprise the staircase. Note the openings at the ends of the hollow girders at the bottom left, which allowed for greater worker access and assembly flexibility.

Opposite: A computer-generated schematic illustrating one piece's positioning in the top staircase level.

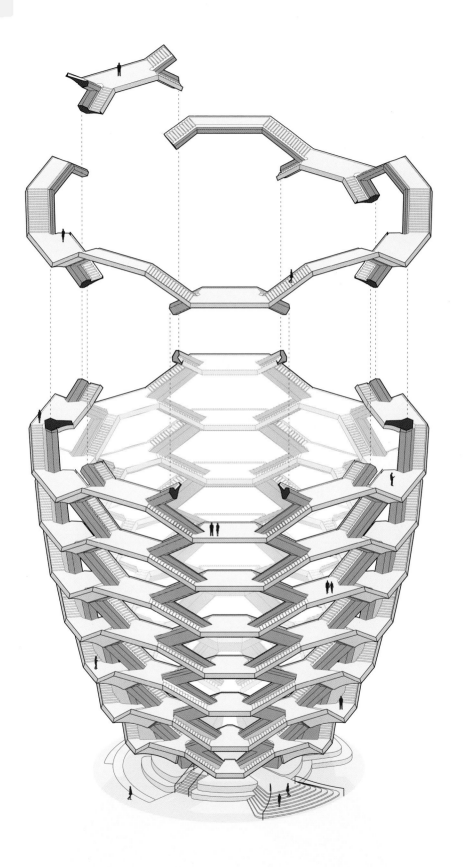

—

If Heatherwick Studio's creation refuses to tell us what to think, it does hint at what we might feel. Its details are in conversation with the environs. The heavy bolts, for instance, echo the venerable metalwork of the High Line, the elevated park that traces the western edge of Hudson Yards.

Consider also the copper color that Heatherwick Studio chose for the cladding. "The surrounding context is primarily steel, glass, and concrete—the language of the city," says Wood, who directed the design with Heatherwick. The shimmering golden-but-not-gold is a response to that: "It feels warm. We felt warmth was important."

From the outside, then, the staircase can seem like an eight-story campfire drawing people to gather. Go within, and the experience takes on another dimension. The highly reflective cladding creates what appears to be a series of screens, dynamic panels that "project" constantly shifting pictures throughout the structure. The metal also reflects the movement of its hundreds of climbers, creating what Heatherwick calls "an object seething with life."

The 154 flights of stairs and 80 accompanying landings do the emotional work: evolutionary psychologists have documented that human beings long to ascend. That said, Heatherwick's intent was not to create foreboding height. Indeed, the staircase comprises one of the shortest structures in Hudson Yards. The feeling he was striving for was less indomitability, more intimacy.

But first the object had to be built.

—

Opposite: A member of Heatherwick Studio holds the completed model.

Overleaf: Models of the structure at various stages of completion.

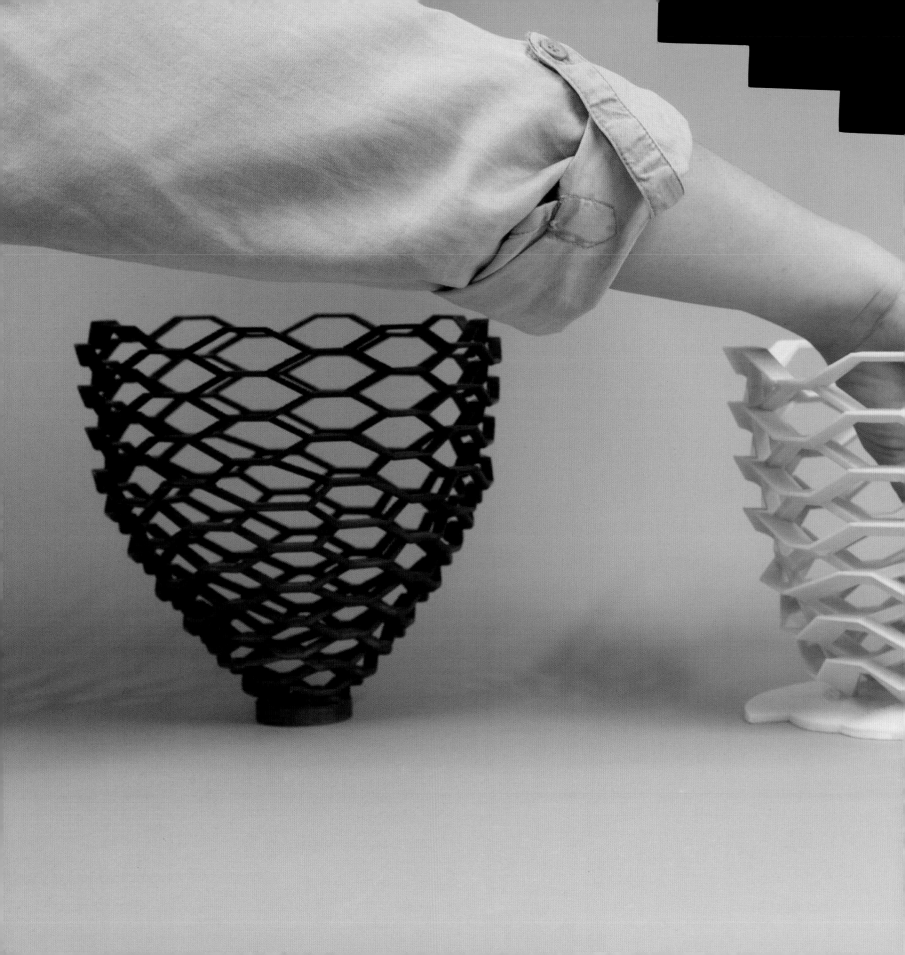

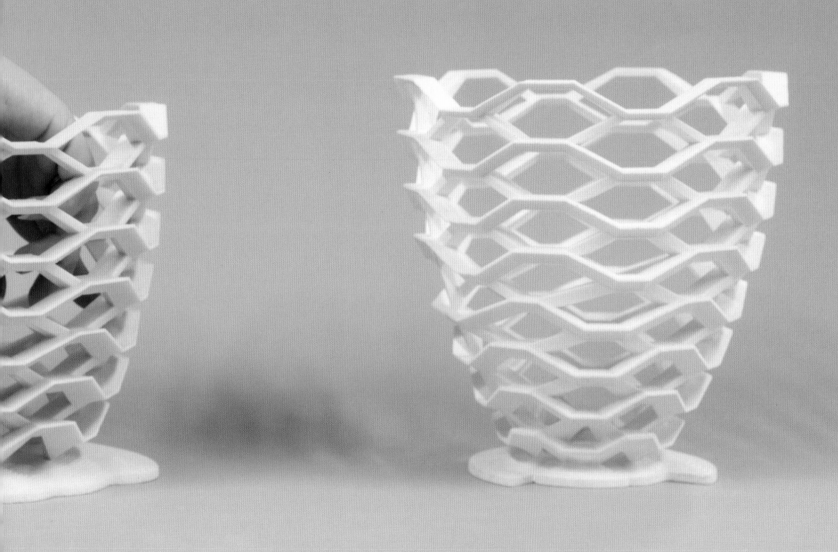

The centerpiece at Hudson Yards was intended to bring people together in one specific spot, but one paradox of its existence is that its journey from conception to completion required the traversing of oceans and a circling of the globe.

A second paradox of the staircase is that an object designed to generate attention was birthed and built in almost total secrecy. All involved went to great lengths to keep the nature and appearance of the design hidden from the public, in part to ensure the greatest impact when it was finally revealed but also because Ross was not interested in what others thought about the Heatherwick idea. "I didn't want to hear anybody's opinion," he says. "I didn't want to be influenced." The cloak-and-dagger efforts ranged from erecting a fence around the outdoor staging area at the staircase fabricator in Europe, to keeping the model and printed version of the Heatherwick Studio slide presentation in a locked cabinet in New York. Ross himself kept the key in his wallet, pulling it out only to show a select few. He keeps the key with him to this day.

Beyond secrecy, among the biggest challenges in bringing the staircase to life involved its most visible element: the copper exterior. Actual copper was out. Exposed to the elements, it quickly grows a green-tinged patina. A consulting metallurgist suggested dozens of possibilities, but all were found wanting for reasons ranging from insufficient reflectivity to poor durability. Finally, the team discovered a solution: a stainless steel treated with a process known as physical vapor deposition (PVD). In PVD, a condensate is turned into a vapor which is then applied to the steel's surface using an electrical charge. Typically, the thin, strong, durable film that results is used for much smaller applications such as hubcaps, drill bits, faucets, or jewelry; its architectural applications are significantly more limited.

The hunt for just the right cladding solution offers a sense of the scope of the challenges involved in making Ross's "Christmas tree" a reality. Every detail—including many that visitors never notice—

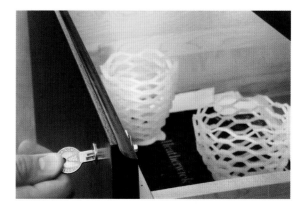

The only key to the top-secret drawer in conference room 18B at the Related offices in New York. In it, Ross kept the early model and slide presentation of the staircase design from prying eyes.

required tremendous thought. Take the guardrails, for example, which receive constant contact but scant attention. One early idea was to cast them as a simple edge of stainless steel or aluminum. But because the structure has no roof and there is little cover from the elements, metal railings would burn skin in summer's heat and winter's cold alike. Wood would offer a layer of warmth, but it would doubtless tempt some visitors to etch "contributions" into it. So the team settled on concrete, a material that tends to go largely unnoticed even as it references the city's urban fabric.

To build this creation, Related and Heatherwick Studio chose the Italian company Cimolai. No stranger to technically demanding projects, Cimolai had recently had a hand in constructing Santiago Calatrava's monumental bridges, as well as the intricate World Cup stadiums in Russia and Qatar. But "this was one of the most complicated projects we've worked on," says Luigi Cimolai, the company's president.

Cimolai's world-class steel milling equipment includes one custom-made, 210-foot machine that is twice as long as most others. The Hudson Yards project put the machines' capabilities to good use. Typically, the task is to fit one piece with another, both with flat surfaces. But, as Luigi Cimolai says, "this was unusual." This work had few flat surfaces. In fact, some of its elements have four milled surfaces that are neither perpendicular to each other nor in conventional positions. The milling machine needed to be able to work in three dimensions. "It was not easy to make—and it's even more difficult to explain," Cimolai says.

To minimize the risk of surprise in Manhattan, the first three levels were preassembled at a Cimolai manufacturing facility in Monfalcone, Italy, near the Slovenian border. The remaining five levels were preassembled, too, in smaller pieces. This painstaking process was to make sure that all the pieces would fit neatly together once transported to New York. According to Claudia Pavan, Cimolai's manager for the project, such preassembly allowed her team to be able to predict every issue.

A welder at work at the Cimolai factory in Monfalcone, Italy.

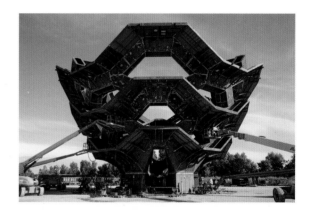

The first three levels preassembled at the Cimolai factory.

A "dog bone" at rest. The preassembled
sections were so nicknamed because of their
resemblance to the canine treat.

The structure was then partly dismantled into large segments—dubbed "dog bones" for their resemblance to the canine treat—so they could be loaded onto cargo ships for the journey. But neither Cimolai nor Related had ever shipped such large yet fragile pieces between continents. None of the cladding, for instance, was more than a fraction of an inch thick; if a section were to be damaged, it couldn't be repaired—it would have to be replaced.

Enter a marine consultant. His job was to envisage the potential risks to the pieces at various points along the way. As he considered how the movement of the seas could affect the ship and the pieces within, the Cimolai-Related team concentrated on protecting the segments during loading and unloading. One option was to custom-make wooden boxes for each dog bone, until it was realized that such packing would add more than $1 million to the budget. Massive polystyrene cushions were considered, then vetoed for environmental reasons. Eventually, the transporters settled on two solutions: bespoke rigging sets with shackles and slings, to counter the variables of each port facility; and preinstalled bumpers and guides to force the pieces to move in predetermined "safe" ways during loading, unloading, and shipping.

Safely aboard the cargo ship, the dog bones traveled from Monfalcone, on the Gulf of Trieste at the northern end of the Adriatic Sea, over the Atlantic to Bayonne, New Jersey. There they were transferred onto barges that crossed the Hudson River, before being transferred again onto flatbed trucks that navigated the streets of Manhattan to Hudson Yards.

Thanks to the meticulous foresight, only one piece was scratched during transit. And the fabrication was so precise that only a single tiny shim was needed during installation. Nevertheless, there were moments that demanded improvisation. For example, when certain pieces were moved into place by telescopic boom lifts, extra protection was called for. The answer came straight from a team member's backyard: foam pool noodles, with their perfect combination of flexibility, cushioning, and affordability.

The dog bones are loaded at a shipyard in Italy before making their transatlantic trip.

The BBC *Norfolk* helped carry dog bones from Italy to New Jersey.

Opposite: The dog bones, which are hollow to allow for worker access, had their openings covered with plywood to keep water out during the oceanic voyage.

Overleaf: A set of dog bones is transported by barge up the Hudson River.

With right angles rare in this Heatherwick Studio creation, the team looked to computer modeling to help resolve the idiosyncratic geometry. But what a machine can render in bits and pixels is not so easily re-rendered in concrete and steel. The varied arcs and doglegs of the stairs and landings mean that all corners are varied, too. And with no two corner moldings alike, each had to be custom-built, a task that demanded a level of precision that not even Cimolai's fabricators had previously deployed.

Another manifestation of those unusual twists and turns is the structure's elevator, for those who cannot navigate the stairs. Elevators, as a rule, approach and leave landings vertically, but what if a structure has few straight lines? In this case, an innovative rack-and-pinion

A set of dog bones safely ensconced in the Hudson Yards "dog pound" and ready for assembly.

Previous: Once ashore, the dog bones were driven down Manhattan's West Side Highway to Hudson Yards.

mechanism inside a massive spine was devised, with a track that alternates between curved and straight sections.

But what was in some ways the most crucial element of the staircase-building process would never be climbed or ridden in any way: the communication required to bring it to life. The Cimolai team, like the crew at Related, understood from the start that this project would demand not just extraordinary technical skills but also an unusual degree of dialogue. "We had to convince our people to go beyond their usual standards," Pavan says.

The need for heightened communication at every stage might be best demonstrated by a moment midway through the journey, as Cimolai and Related considered what to tell the dockworkers who would handle the pieces at every port. "They're used to heavy stuff, a lot of steel," Pavan explains. "If they're given a piece of paper that says they're handling bulk steel, they'll treat it like bulk steel." Tugboat captains also received lengthy memos to explain the against-appearances delicacy of the dog bones.

Foam pool noodles were the low-tech solution to the problem of how to protect the delicate surfaces from construction dings and dents.

Communications were complicated by the number of nationalities of the people involved. It would be a mistake to view the making of the staircase as a feat of creativity, engineering, transportation, and construction without acknowledging the hands and minds that created, engineered, transported, and constructed it. These included not just the British designers, Italian fabricators, and American developers and construction workers, but also Spanish steelmakers, Croatian glassworkers, Canadian wind-tunnel testers, German engineers, and even that one guy of unknown nationality wearing a GoPro camera, who mapped out the last-leg truck route in Manhattan on his bike. None had ever worked on anything like this before. Indeed, the staircase accomplished in its creation the very thing that Heatherwick expected: it brought a diverse group of people together for a unique experience.

So, yes, it is a basket and a pineapple and a riddle. But those who see a beehive may be closest to its essence. Like a hive, it is inside that the alchemy occurs. Then again, it has always been impossible to predict how visitors will respond. "You're free to experience it and make up your own mind," Heatherwick says. "New things happen to us when we're not supposed to be solving problems but just creating excuses to play."

The design of an object is fulfilled only in its use—a song must be sung, a play acted, a painting seen. Although thousands of people contributed to the making of the staircase, untold thousands more bring it to life every day. Every visitor is, in a sense, a co-creator.

Detailed modeling and precise engineering have prepared the way for them all, calculating the structure's response to the climbing crowds. Systems of weights and springs, each weighing approximately 13 tons, have been embedded in the floors of the top three levels. They serve as giant dampers that absorb the footsteps and harmonize the ever-changing symphony of vibrations. Because we misunderstand this unique object if we consider it only from afar. A promenade is nothing without people walking on it. This plaza anchor, this centerpiece, was designed to be entered and experienced. Although seemingly a finished and static thing, its essence is—and will always be—animation.

Opposite: A worker maneuvers a dog bone
into position.

Above: The staircase rests on six foundational pieces that were incorporated into the platform below, itself built above a working rail yard.

Left: It took eight months in total to top out the structure, but the actual time required to lift and secure each of the 81 dog bones was mere minutes. Far more time was spent in preparation for each hoist and placement.

Although different types of cranes and positioning methods
were considered, the structure was eventually built
from the inside out, using a crane placed in its middle.

Engineering

as precise as it is

complex, as original as

it is

elegant.

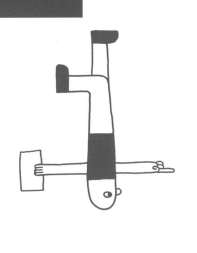

FABRICATION

It is appropriate, if not poetic, that a monument intended as a unique twenty-first-century greeting was constructed in a uniquely twenty-first-century manner. As with the Statue of Liberty a few miles to its south, the centerpiece of Hudson Yards was designed and built in Europe. But unlike the straight-line origin of the Lady in the Harbor, fabricating the staircase involved materials sourced, techniques applied, and assembly undertaken in half a dozen countries on three different continents. Its creation was a feat of cooperation and engineering as precise as it was complex, as original as it was elegant.

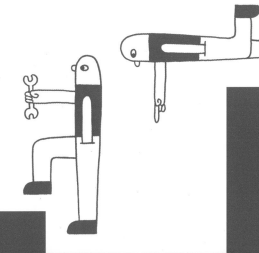

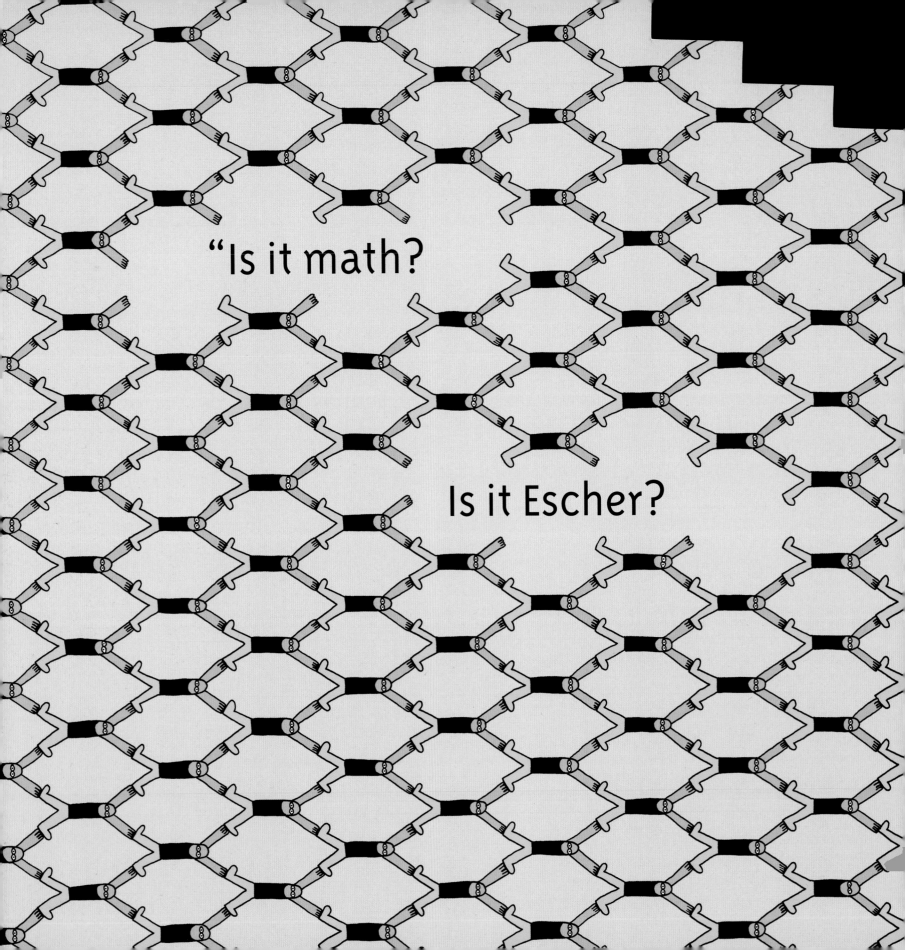

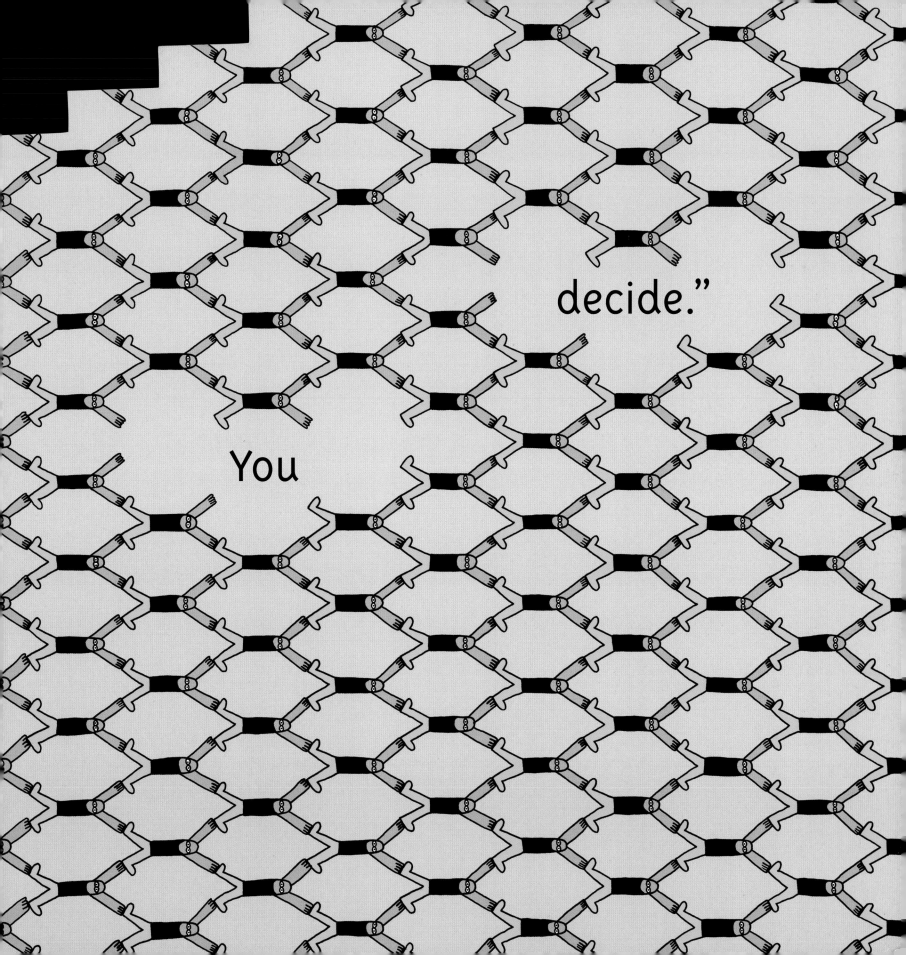

You

decide."

A 5,000-mile
relay by the most
eclectic collection
of conveyances.

TRANSPORTATION

If the technical matter of manufacturing the staircase was daunting, the logistical challenge of getting it from Europe to North America was confounding. Rarely if ever has a package so valuable, so unusually shaped, and so easily damaged been ferried such distances, across such different terrain. To mitigate the possibility of catastrophe, the design, construction, and assembly teams agreed to transport the piece in dozens of individually cocooned smaller sections throughout its 5,000-mile relay from Monfalcone, Italy, to New York City. The trip's short hops and long voyages required their own eclectic collection of conveyances—self-propelled modular transporters and cargo ships, river barges and flat-bed trucks, forklifts and cranes.

A WEST SIDE STORY

HUDSON YARDS,
THE NEW HEART OF
NEW YORK

—

Sarah Medford

In *Here Is New York*, a 1948 ode to the city and its inhabitants, E. B. White suggested that "Manhattan has been compelled to advance skyward because of the absence of any other direction in which to grow." White was a keen, if slightly cantankerous, urban observer, but Hudson Yards is proof that New York had more up its sleeve than he—or anyone else—realized. Well into the twenty-first century, Manhattan has a new 28-acre neighborhood, spanning four city blocks north to south and running east to west from Tenth Avenue to the Hudson River. Here is New York descending, too: beneath the glassy towers, the world's busiest working rail yard shuttles trains back and forth to Long Island.

Of course, New York has always had an element of stagecraft about it. Even the idea of mounting a new city atop a platform has a distinctly theatrical feeling. But the brawny reality of Hudson Yards stands up and out for all to see. Stephen Ross, chairman of Related Companies, the project's co-developer, calls it "the new heart of New York," and the master plan bears this out: an eventual 18 million square feet of commercial and residential space spread across sixteen buildings; abundant shopping and dining options, including an expansive gourmet market from star chef José Andrés; and The Shed, a cultural center as notable for its innovative design as it will be for its multimedia exhibitions.

It might be that White didn't register this part of town in his literary accounting because it had been marginalized for so long. A low-lying industrial swath, it was a virtual no-man's land seven decades ago when he sat down to write. A few centuries earlier, it wasn't even that: not land at all, just water. Much of the western edge of today's Manhattan Island was reclaimed over time from marsh and scrub forest.

But today that reclamation is little more than a memory. Along with the extension of the No. 7 subway line, Hudson Yards has been a major catalyst for a wider development and construction renaissance

The Gansevoort Market in Manhattan's Meatpacking District circa 1900. Today, this area is at the southern end of a major West Side development that includes Hudson Yards.

Opposite: Manhattan's West Side rail yards in the early construction days of the Hudson Yards platform.

on Manhattan's West Side. This frenzy of commercial and residential activity includes a dozen surrounding projects, connecting the Hell's Kitchen neighborhood and Times Square to the north with Chelsea to the south. Furthering this cohesion is Hudson River Park, the High Line, Hudson Park & Boulevard, and several other green spaces and recreational oases—some already completed, others under development—that extend from the Meatpacking District all the way to Midtown. All of it contributes to a coherent West Side, for the first time ever.

But as broad and dramatic as this transformation has been, it is not unprecedented in the city's history. Indeed, the previous century saw the evolution of similar signature projects—not just buildings and infrastructure, but destinations with a certain nobility and romance: Rockefeller Center, Lincoln Center, the United Nations Headquarters. Like Hudson Yards, each is a porous arrangement, open to the rest of the city and welcoming to passersby. And each has its own character, determined by elements as diverse as the public art on display or the reasons people are compelled to be there. Hudson Yards is the latest iteration of New York's pulse-quickening gift for reinvention.

The Hudson River Railway in 1859. Connecting New York City and Albany, its tracks ran along Tenth and Eleventh avenues, past present-day Hudson Yards.

Opposite: A 1934 aerial view of the elevated rail line that replaced the hazardous street-level tracks of the Hudson River Railway—and later was transformed into the elevated park known as the High Line.

Like many things within it—dogs, cars, restaurants—New York seems increasingly to come in only two sizes: tiny or colossal. It's difficult to fully appreciate the totality of Hudson Yards without some distance—a few blocks at least, or better yet a trip out on the Hudson River. But another place to gain understanding of the scale shift underway in Hudson Yards, and with it the inevitable shift of heart and mind, is on the fringes of this new neighborhood. Just down the street, the local scene registers the progress.

Each day at noon, the door of Death Avenue opens to admit the first rush of the lunch crowd. The bartender there happily explains that

The Pennsylvania Railroad Station and rail yard
circa 1915. The tracks under Hudson Yards, two blocks
to the west, still connect to this busy commuter hub.

Overleaf: William Connolly,
the "Eleventh Avenue Cowboy," does the best he can
to conduct city traffic on horseback in 1932.

the restaurant's portentous name refers to its location along a particular stretch of Tenth Avenue made murderous by the train that raced down its center.

For centuries, Manhattan's West Side welcomed a succession of rough cliques: soldiers in military encampments, workers at the slaughterhouses, and, of course, railmen. In the 1850s, a flourishing freight line that extended as far north as Albany, the state capital, was a particular kind of traffic problem for the pedestrians in the neighborhood. These trains may have delivered butter and eggs to nearly one million city dwellers, but they also put many of those lives at risk. For this reason, "cowboys" on horseback trotted ahead of the trains in an effort to keep people off the tracks. They were not always successful: over the years, hundreds died and countless more were injured.

In 1934, decades-long talk of an elevated rail line finally became reality, and the High Line, a railway spur since converted into a park, facilitated its initial delivery. That wasn't the first engineering feat in the area, however. In 1910, the Pennsylvania Railroad had succeeded in boring through the silt beneath the miles-wide Hudson to construct its North River Tunnels. Those underground tubes, which delivered trains to the original Penn Station, are still in use today. The groundbreaking for this particular "big dig" began in what is now the center of Hudson Yards' public square.

In the lobby of 475 Tenth Avenue, a white terra-cotta office building on the northeastern edge of Hudson Yards, silver-toned prints by photographer Lewis Hine capture scenes of industrial might from the 1920s, only a few years after the building opened for business. Oversized windows—and a Siberian location as far as leasing agents were concerned—made the address an affordable and popular home to architecture offices for decades. Now only two or three remain, the others having been replaced by tech companies, hotel groups, and fashion brands. An art gallery occupies the ground-floor space. "The neighborhood—it never stays the same," says a guard at the front desk;

"This used to be the last frontier, but now…" He slices the air with a few quick strokes.

Things have changed.

━━━

How do the people who work in the neighborhood get there? One answer lies beneath the petal-shaped roof of the No. 7 subway station, which rises on 34th Street between Tenth and Eleventh avenues like something out of *Battlestar Galactica*. Below ground, a steady human wave pushes through the turnstiles into a cavernous chamber serviced by a digital billboard that rotates through ads every few seconds. There is no trash—and no trash cans. What catches the eye are the friendly Scandinavian-modern dock lights above each turnstile. A worker in a spotless neon vest explains that they aren't lights but cameras, and he puts the number of them station-wide at around three hundred—"for your safety," he adds with a smile. Hudson Yards is no loose end of the system. Think of it more as a recirculating hub.

The No. 7 train made its first trip from here in September 2015, almost two decades and $2.4 billion after the extension was proposed. When commuters and tourists step off the escalators that bring them to street level, the scene that greets them is an iteration or two beyond what Mayor Rudy Giuliani imagined in the 1990s: a baseball stadium built above the rail yards. A decade earlier, the yards had been designed—with foresight by the Metropolitan Transportation Authority (MTA)—to allow for the insertion of three hundred caissons, or structural supports, between the tracks at a density great enough to hold whatever the future might have in mind.

Although the ballpark concept faded soon enough, it was followed by even bigger talk: of a main stadium for the 2012 Olympic Games, to be converted afterwards into a home for the New York Jets. But the city's Olympic bid lost to London's, and local voters turned out to be lukewarm

The No. 7 subway line extension stops at West 34th Street and Eleventh Avenue, at the front door of Hudson Yards.

Above: Underground construction of the No. 7 subway line extension at Hudson Yards.

Left: A view east from Eleventh Avenue over the working rail yards.

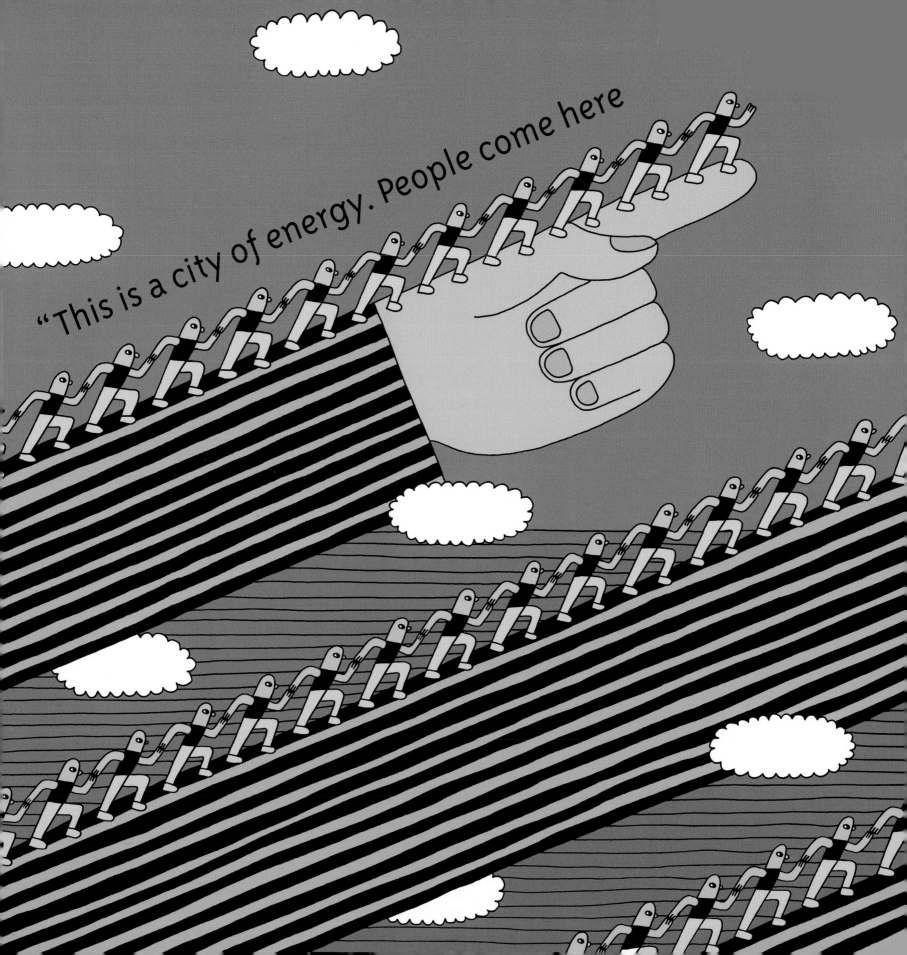

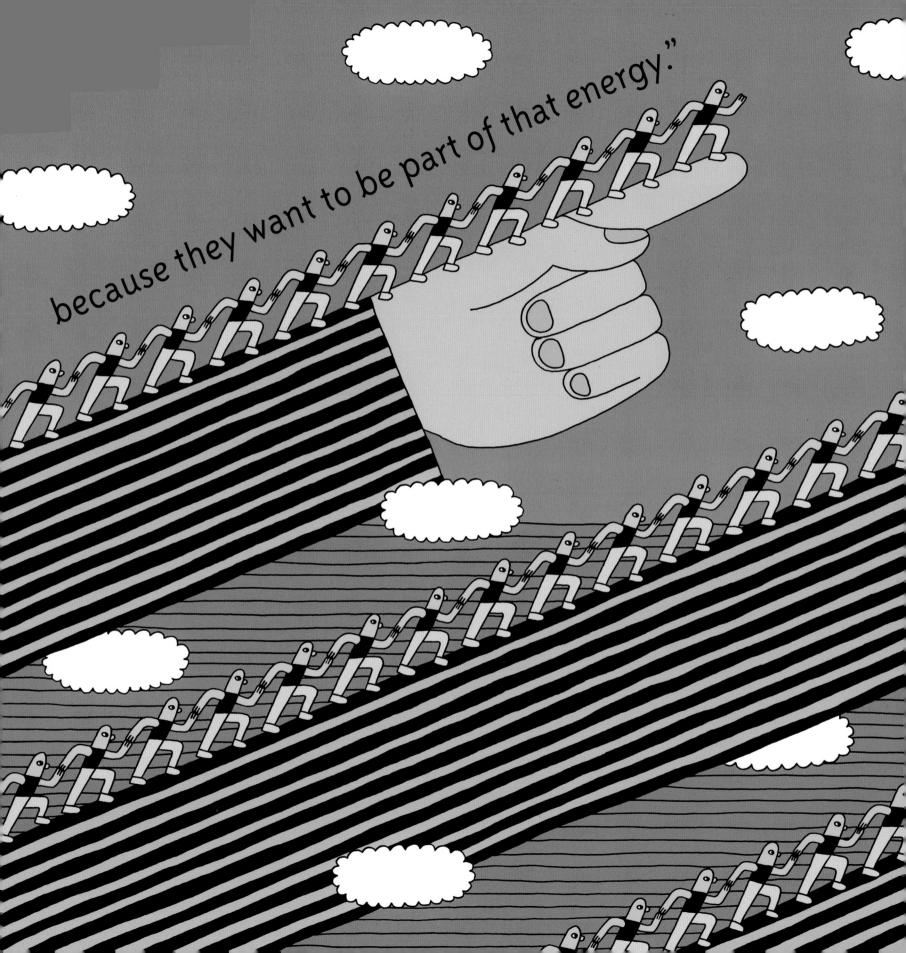

toward professional football in Manhattan. Nonetheless, a spotlight
now shone on the rail yard and its environs. That spotlight brightened
considerably in 2001, when a panel of thirty-five experts assembled by
US Senator Chuck Schumer proposed the creation of 60 million square
feet of office space and a subway extension for the West Side.

Dan Doctoroff, chairman of The Shed, led the failed Olympic bid
and thus has lived with the idea of what Hudson Yards could be for
longer than many of its tenants have been alive. As deputy mayor under
Michael Bloomberg in the early years of this century, Doctoroff led a
local effort to sketch out a vision for growth that would keep New York
City globally competitive in the twenty-first century. Central to the
plan was the development of Midtown's West Side.

At the time, he and his team were working with something close
to a blank canvas. "When we started, there were just eleven residences
registered with the city between 30th and 42nd streets, from Tenth
Avenue to the river," he says. "A couple of buildings of a few stories
each. Tax revenue had actually gone *down* in the area over time.
And there were fewer trees and shrubs than anywhere else in the city.
There was no uprooting of old New York because nothing was here."

In 2005, as the city recovered its financial footing following the
2001 recession and 9/11 attacks, a rezoning plan was finally approved
and the door was opened to office and residential use. In 2008, after a
process to choose a developer saw the initial winner back out, Related
signed a deal with the MTA to lease the air rights over the rail yards
and promptly set to work building something that would bring the city
and its citizens westward. A daring proposition even in steady economic
times, the arrangement seemed positively perilous in the midst of the
latest global financial shakedown. But Stephen Ross was confident that
an urban mixed-use development designed for the future would not fail.

Related turned for inspiration to grand civic projects like Rockefeller
Center. From the start, it was clear that Ross and his crew shared a
bit of the showmanship expressed by Samuel "Roxy" Rothafel, creator

of Radio City Music Hall, who declared: "Don't give the people what they want, give 'em something better." The towers built at Hudson Yards are some of the biggest and boldest the world has seen.

Three of them were designed by architecture firm Kohn Pedersen Fox (KPF), who also led the master-planning effort of the entire development. KPF principal William Pedersen worked from the premise that "scale creates energy, and dynamism creates energy of another order." He is not at all surprised that the extreme contrasts that currently animate Manhattan's western edge continue to act as "a generator that is making Hudson Yards a success."

A century ago, the layout of Hudson Yards as it is today might have been described as the spokes of a wheel, its buildings forming a loose circle around the Heatherwick Studio-designed staircase in the middle. But a better, more contemporary analogy might be a central charging station, powering up the 125,000 daily residents of, and visitors to, this new town square.

How did the West Side transform from a place where vitality had drained away to the destination it is today? It didn't hurt that local government and the private sector shared a vision of the future. It also didn't hurt that this was New York City. "This is a city of energy," says Ross, who was born and raised in Michigan and moved to New York a half-century ago to pursue his dreams. "It attracts the best and the brightest. People come here because they want to be part of that energy."

A similar dynamic played out among the commercial tenants relocating to the area. As top-tier firms from one sector leased space, those in others followed; in Hudson Yards proper, companies that have made long-term commitments include entertainment conglomerate WarnerMedia; software corporation SAP; fashion company Tapestry; investment firm BlackRock; law firm Milbank LLP; cosmetics maker L'Oreal; and retailer Neiman-Marcus. More industry leaders are signing up to buildings farther from the neighborhood's core. The commercial and cultural promise of "Midtown West" is well on its way to being fulfilled.

The High Line at sunset.

Up on the High Line, a new community takes shape each day. Puffer coat-wearing hipsters and visiting families from around the globe, pedestrian commuters, couples with their strollered kids, men in brogues and women in snub-toed clogs—all of them travel as one on the reimagined rail system that connects Hudson Yards to points south. The man-made landscape between Ninth and Tenth avenues is mostly unchanged. Dogwoods flower on the brownstone blocks, and stately brick factory buildings have been renovated for new uses. Both were spared when the decision was made not to rezone this north–south corridor, all but guaranteeing that the patchwork fabric of this part of town would be retained.

New York "carries on its lapel the unexpungeable odor of the long past," White wrote in his essay. Also the scent of a freshly unearthed discovery.

Out on the river, a prime stateroom on the *Norwegian Bliss* cruise ship puts a traveler at roughly the same elevation as a corner-office executive on a lower floor of 55 Hudson Yards. Even from this distance, Heatherwick Studio's centerpiece sculpture holds the eye, though the swarms of climbers on it look smaller than ants on a cupcake. High above it, the glass-and-steel observation deck juts out from 30 Hudson Yards, a cocked elbow at 1,100 feet. Architect Pedersen's triangular prow works in tandem with Heatherwick's staircase. "These are the two primary civic gestures of Hudson Yards," Pedersen says. "One is outward-facing, the opposite of the other, which is really internalized." The soaring viewing platform faces east down 34th Street toward the Empire State Building, and south to its sister tower 10 Hudson Yards. Pedersen conceived of these two towers as being in conversation. "I've always thought of a master plan as a cocktail party, with the buildings as guests," he says. "Buildings can be in dialogue with each other. This is an essay in a very specific attitude."

Another type of conversation is taking place down below, where mature willow oaks and American elms can't begin to reach the sharply dressed party guests in the sky. Nature is the mediator here, providing a human-scale reference amid buildings that stretch to almost unimaginable heights. This is the domain of Thomas Woltz of Nelson Byrd Woltz, the neighborhood's landscape architect, who laid a soil bed above a rail yard and then devised a cooling system that keeps the soil temperature below 75 degrees even on sweltering days. The hundreds of trees Woltz's team planted yield a green haven that guarantees a future alive in more ways than one. "We've used tools of immersion and lyrical composition to create a voice for the public space that holds up in the context," he says. "We hope people will build a lasting relationship with this space and see it as a new center for ritual, play, and daily life."

Some of those play options are indoors. An art lover can arrive at Hudson Yards on foot from one of the Chelsea galleries to check out permanent installations by Frank Stella or Jaume Plensa, or catch a performance at The Shed. On weekday evenings, kids and commuters heading south from the subway pause in the square for a chocolate chip cookie or sit for a minute to let the breeze off the water revive them.

In *Here Is New York*, White noted nearly a hundred locations around town by name, from the Algonquin Hotel and the Third Avenue Elevated to Cherry Street on the Lower East Side. Although the new West Side couldn't have been among them, it surely would have pleased White to know that the outdoor concerts he enjoyed are now hosted in a tree-shaded park here, while eons-old New York granite supports a climbable sculpture that can be seen as an ode to young strivers pursuing a never-before-seen view and a newly imagined future.

Overleaf: Heatherwick Studio's creation in all
its glory in the first weeks after opening.

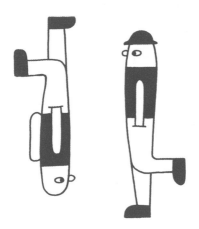

This monument realizes the hopes of its creators, reinventing

itself every second

of every day.

REACTION

History will render more profound judgments on the visual appeal and civic impact of the staircase, but the verdict already issued by the waves of visitors drawn to Hudson Yards in the first dawns of its public life could not be more clear. Instantly a social media phenomenon, the insistently interactive monument clearly realizes the vision and hopes of its creators. Deluged by thousands of visitors daily, it reinvents itself by the second, whenever a single soul—or hundreds of them—climbs its flights and pauses on its landings. Every look up (or down), every gaze out (or in), every smile shared with a companion (or stranger) is further confirmation of Ross's original vision.

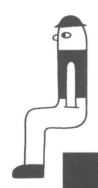

MOVEMENT

AS

MONUMENT

A
TWENTY-FIRST-CENTURY
PUBLIC SPACE

Paul Goldberger

If there is anything that distinguishes public space of the twenty-first century it is a focus on movement. You could say that these spaces are designed to elevate engagement over contemplation. Our time produces the High Line, an urban promenade intimately intertwined with its city, while the nineteenth century gave us Central Park, a smorgasbord of natural landscapes conceived to make the city disappear. The High Line's meaning is only revealed as you move along it and look outward, seeing New York from constantly changing vantage points; Central Park is most deeply experienced when you stop, struck by any one of the sublime compositions of its designers, Frederick Law Olmsted and Calvert Vaux. For all its genius, Central Park emerged from an age that did not trust that the urban form by itself could provide citizens with leisure; it was made as an Edenic alternative to harsh streets. To enter Central Park is to leave the city behind. But today we do not want to leave the city behind. The High Line was not made to be an escape from the streets. It *is* a street, offering not a release from urban experience but a gentler version of it.

A gentler version of urban experience is also a fair description of the intention of the public space at the heart of Hudson Yards, with its 150-foot-high centerpiece that carries the notion of movement to an extreme. However striking it may be to look at, it was designed to be climbed. One must walk its intricate honeycomb of 154 crisscrossing staircases, inventing a route as you go, in order to thoroughly appreciate it.

The Public Square and Gardens, as the entire open space at the heart of Hudson Yards is officially named, is an amalgam of the classic notion of the park and the twenty-first century's evolving vision of the public space. A square is, in its essence, a celebration of urbanity, not a retreat from it. But, at the same time, the presence of nature within the city remains as seductive as it was in Olmsted's day. The challenge is to integrate the two—to make a space that encourages engagement while providing relief from the pressures that come from too much urbanity and not enough green, too much construction and not enough sky.

The High Line epitomizes a new notion of public space that encourages movement and activity.

Central Park represents the nineteenth-century ideal of public space as a natural landscape that offers respite from bustling urban life.

Opposite: From the moment it opened, the staircase was a magnet for visitors of all ages.

As designed by the landscape architecture firm Nelson Byrd Woltz, the Public Square and Gardens is no island of green set apart from Manhattan's streets and buildings. Instead, it blurs the distinction, separating one from the other with markers and bollards, not pavement and curbs. The goal, partner Thomas Woltz has said, was to use the landscape as "a middle ground, the stitch between all of the different buildings and streets that surround the plaza space."

It is worth noting that New York City actually has few urban squares. It is, to be sure, full of places called "squares"—Herald Square, Verdi Square, Greeley Square, Lincoln Square—that exist where the diagonal Broadway stem crosses one of the city grid's avenues, but they tend to be more like little parks, often awkwardly shaped. Though reasonable enough places in themselves, they lack any of the qualities that define a major civic square, which is to say they are not filled with people, activity, or an aspiration to some grandeur. A great square is

The public space at Hudson Yards, like Times Square, is not an urban square in the classic sense but is nonetheless a lively global crossroads.

Above: Laurie Olin's redesign of Midtown Manhattan's Bryant Park. At Hudson Yards, landscape architect Thomas Woltz also used arboreal touches to create a haven for urban naturalists.

Left: Hudson Yards' Public Square echoes the world-renowned Lincoln Center Plaza in that it is defined by the buildings around it and the culture lovers who fill it.

"This century has little patience for objects it can't explore."

really an outdoor room, one whose walls are the surrounding buildings and whose ceiling is the sky. By that measure, perhaps only three places in Manhattan—Rockefeller Center; Lincoln Center Plaza; and Bryant Park, behind the New York Public Library—qualify. And while the last two of these have been updated over the past generation with welcome jolts of improved design, none can be described as a twenty-first-century urban square.

For that, one must look to what has taken shape at Hudson Yards. In this new neighborhood, the combination of landscape and sculptural-architectural invention has resulted in a public space that aspires to join the elements of a traditional, monumental civic space to the modern love of activity. And the object in the center is the main attraction, in part because it was not randomly placed; everything about the public space sets off the striking assemblage of 2,500 stairs created by the London-based Heatherwick Studio.

Like all successful squares, this one, too, is a room, defined by the buildings around it. But we are a far cry from the genteel surroundings of the Place Vendôme or Place des Vosges in Paris. The first indication that this is a civic space in the new millennium is the scale of the bordering towers, an intentionally varied collection designed by Kohn Pedersen Fox; David Childs with Skidmore, Owings & Merrill; and Diller Scofidio + Renfro. (The Shed, the new cultural facility designed by Diller Scofidio + Renfro and Rockwell Group, and a shopping and restaurant complex designed by Elkus Manfredi Architects with Kohn Pedersen Fox complete the frame.) They are huge, far bigger than those of Rockefeller Center, the design benchmark by which all multi-tower, multi-use urban developments are measured. Given the scale of Hudson Yards, the 5-acre open space in its midst could easily have felt as bereft of life as the plaza that once existed beneath the twin towers of the original World Trade Center—more empty podium than bustling square. Designing a viable public space is no simple task; there are few successful models at this scale. More challenging still, the public space

The Place Vendôme in Paris has a monumental column—erected by Napoleon I to commemorate the Battle of Austerlitz—as its focal point.

The Place des Vosges, the oldest planned square in Paris, is at once an intimate park and a monumental urban square.

at Hudson Yards is not even a square in the literal sense, but rather a large "L" open to both the east and north.

Where is the center of an L? The planners saw it as the point where the two rectangles overlap—the hinge, as it were, of the space, that helps it to turn the corner. Woltz's layout of intersecting, unevenly sized ellipses does some work here. By appearing to rotate around the hinge, the ellipses emphasize its centrality.

As for what would define that hinge, Stephen Ross, chairman of Related Companies, co-developer of the site, felt strongly that it should not be a conventional piece of sculpture blown up to enormous dimensions. Nor did he want an object that would only be stared at. Ross wanted something that he had never seen before, something that would encourage engagement. For his part, Thomas Heatherwick, who has a reputation as a master of surprise—he is the leader of a London design studio known for responding to challenges in fresh and theatrical ways—understood that the scale of the outdoor space at Hudson Yards was not necessarily conducive to human interaction. "We saw our role as making a catalyst," he says. Whatever ended up in the center of the plaza, he reasoned, must feel substantial enough to provide a focal point in the midst of the huge buildings. But at the same time, it had to be both transparent enough not to swallow the surrounding space or overwhelm the gardens, and magnetic enough to pull people toward it.

What Heatherwick and the studio created definitely pulls people toward it. It pulls them into, up, and all around it as well. The staircase is at once a piece of architecture, a piece of sculpture, and an urban symbol. Unlike most urban symbols, though, this one is an object of play. Its multifaceted quality may frustrate the makers of monumental urban sculpture who try to involve people emotionally but rarely succeed in doing so. Here, Heatherwick has made engagement not merely possible but inevitable. To see his piece is to want to plunge right in and start climbing. When the landings are busy with people,

Man-made flights of fancy, like the first Ferris wheel (built for the 1893 Chicago World's Fair), have always drawn crowds.

Two hundred years ago, the short-lived Promenades Aériennes,
set in the amusement park surroundings of the
Jardin Beaujon in Paris, was an early proof of concept
for public monument as interactive endeavor.

the object looks like a gargantuan beehive, combining the strolling ease of the Italian *passeggiata*, the energy of a workout, and the formidable presence of a monument.

Heatherwick Studio compare their assemblage of stairways to ancient Indian stepwells, although its glittery metallic sheathing is a far cry from the solid stone versions that go down into the earth rather than up toward the sky. In its complexity and many alternating paths, the object suggests a connection to labyrinths, even though in its transparency it is exactly the opposite of a labyrinth: you cannot get lost among these landings. Because nothing is enclosed, you can always see in and out and up and down. There is no wrong way to ascend or descend, and there are no dead ends or blocked routes. It is labyrinth-turned-carefree-game, the player's vista shifting with every step. If most visitors choose to climb to the top, the view from there, while most expansive, is focused outward by virtue of the structure's splaying, bowl-like shape. The more exciting vantage point is actually in the middle

The Trylon and Perisphere, built for the 1939 New York World's Fair.

Opposite: Heatherwick Studio's Seed Cathedral, which served as the UK Pavilion at the Shanghai World Expo in 2010. Like the Trylon and Perisphere, it was dismantled once the events were over.

of the bowl, because you look inward as much as outward. That's where you feel most enmeshed in Heatherwick Studio's wild doodle.

It is hard not to think that another side to the object's ancestry lies in a genre of inventive structures that have little physical resemblance to the design but feel even more connected to it in spirit than the Indian stepwells: those flights of fancy built to symbolize and celebrate world's fairs—the Eiffel Tower from the Paris Exposition of 1889, the Ferris Wheel from the World's Columbian Exposition in Chicago of 1893, the Trylon and Perisphere from the New York World's Fair of 1939, and the Unisphere from the New York World's Fair of 1964. None of these are conventional buildings, yet each is a formidable architectural presence. Heatherwick's widely admired Seed Cathedral, the UK pavilion at Shanghai's Expo 2010, made clear how at home he felt working in this genre, in which a conventional building program gives way to something more exotic, freed from many of architecture's usual constraints.

Most world's fair structures are temporary—the Seed Cathedral was dismantled after the Expo—but some have become lasting symbols of their cities, and none more so than the Eiffel Tower. In time, a city confers iconicity on its monuments. When the tower was new there was nothing Parisian about it—indeed, the more sophisticated critics of the time resented it as a vulgar intrusion, a dramatic sign of a modernity that they believed was destroying the city they knew. Now, of course, the tower is beloved, the structure more identified with Paris than any other. So too with another world's fair construction, less famous but bearing a closer resemblance to the Hudson Yards centerpiece, at least in scale: the Atomium from the 1958 Brussels World's Fair, a 335-foot-high set of nine intersecting spheres that represent the atoms in a single unit of iron crystal, blown up to 165 billion times its actual size. The Atomium's form had no more innate connection to Brussels than Eiffel's iron construction had to its city, and yet, over time, both became cherished civic symbols.

The Atomium, constructed for the Brussels World's Fair in 1958, is perhaps the most identifiable symbol of the city today.

It is a fallacy to believe that successful symbols only reflect a city's character; sometimes they contribute their own qualities, gradually shaping a city's identity rather than simply mirroring it. Yet another kind of precedent for Heatherwick Studio's staircase is Philip Johnson and John Burgee's Fort Worth Water Gardens of 1974, a series of stepped terraces and fountains built as a downtown renewal project. Creating a space that people feel compelled to explore, it is one of the rare public pieces from the Brutalist 1970s that encourages engagement.

Heatherwick Studio's creation, like the Atomium, Water Gardens, and Eiffel Tower, is a conflation of sculpture and architecture, abstract enough to be perceived first as a shape and only second as functional object. It shares some other qualities with these places as well. For one thing, it was designed to be entered and explored. Although it does not contain interior space like the Atomium or the Eiffel Tower, it is largely transparent, as they are, reading as a framework that punctuates the space it occupies rather than overwhelming it. But today, when the expectations for public space are centered around activity and engagement, a structure with a transparent framework would not have been sufficient to serve as a centerpiece for Hudson Yards, not if it could be viewed only from afar, like the 1964 New York World's Fair's Unisphere. The twenty-first century has little patience for objects it cannot explore. As for the more conventional option of anchoring the space with a work of pure sculpture, the scale of Hudson Yards, defined as much by the powerful verticality of its towers as by the square footage on the ground, would have swallowed even the largest work. Something that was similar to a work of architecture, but not quite a building, was called for.

Only time has the power to grant true iconic status to this assemblage of staircases, but the structure's seemingly infinite number of paths does seem to be a perfect metaphor for New York City. You make your way up and around it as you want; each stairway brings you to a landing where you choose between three others or the one you just climbed.

The Fort Worth Water Gardens, completed in 1974, was designed to encourage visitors to move around and through it.

You decide again and again whether to move up or down, clockwise or counterclockwise, forward or backward. It is utterly non linear, a celebration of choice in which there is no right way or wrong way, and everything leads eventually to the top, until you decide to turn back. The object is designed to encourage you to climb, to walk, to move.

Other than the Statue of Liberty, New York's architectural icons have always been its skyscrapers. It makes a certain amount of sense that New York, the city that treats work as pleasure, has long taken office towers as its most celebrated symbols. Heatherwick Studio's creation was not conceived to replace the Chrysler Building in the hearts of New Yorkers, but to be a new and different kind of symbol. The piece falls into a category that, at least in New York, it will have almost to itself. It is neither monument nor memorial; it commemorates no historical event. It is not a seat of government or a commercial building.

You could say, in fact, that what this new landmark actually belongs to is the long and honorable tradition of structures built primarily to bring pleasure, the building type historically known as the "architectural folly"—a curious and unjust term, because it can be wrongly taken to suggest something trivial. In reality, these structures frequently bring us closer to serious architectural experience than conventional buildings do. Ours is primarily an age of business; we rarely build solely for pleasure.

Not the least of the virtues of the Hudson Yards centerpiece, then, is that it forces us to think again about the possibilities that architecture holds for us when its purpose is not to contain rentable space or to awe us with spatial and structural gymnastics, but simply to be delightful to look at and enticing to explore. Follies are expressions of pleasure, and this staircase is, in the end, exactly that— a pleasure, to behold and to experience. This act of exuberance takes on the challenge of place-making by punctuating Hudson Yards with an exclamation of joy.

Opposite: Now a beloved symbol of its city, Gustave Eiffel's famous tower was not at first well received when it was erected as the centerpiece of the 1889 Paris Exposition.

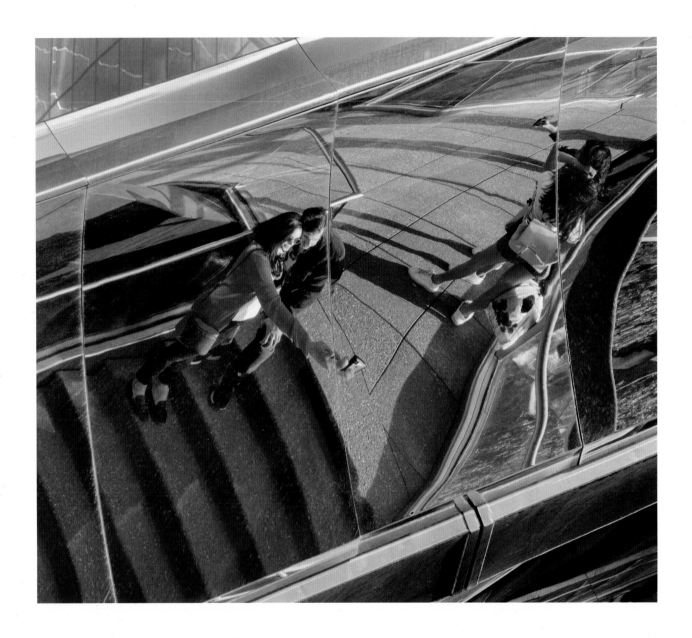

Media Darling

From its debut, visitors found the staircase to be an infinitely ripe subject
for visual interpretation and a unique stage for individual expression,
whether on social media or by other means.

⃝ @themayotv

⃝ @walthaim

⃝ @marvinlei

⃝ @shadyblackdog

⃝ @yogini9o

⃝ @anniecroll_

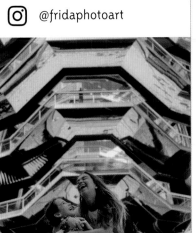

@fridaphotoart

@frederic_lere

@floraracama

@jnpersonalizations

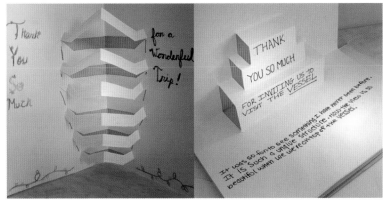

Notes to the developer from NYC Lab Middle School students
after a visit to the staircase.

If the staircase were a bowl, it could hold

If you laid the 30,150 or so bolts used to secure the staircases end to end, at 3.6 miles they'd just about reach from one end of the Las Vegas Strip to the other.

The 232 days it took to raise the structure to its full height of 150 feet is about the same as the gestation period of a polar bear.

If all 154 flights of stairs were stacked vertically, they'd carry you to about the 65th floor of the Empire State Building.

At 3,200 tons, the staircase weighs as much as fourteen Statues of Liberty—but only one-third of an Eiffel Tower.

The amount of glass in the structure (31,951 square feet) is roughly equivalent to that used to make the Louvre Pyramid in Paris.

Olympic swimming pools of water.

The 4,000 gallons of paint used on the staircase could be used to repaint the White House almost seven times.

about thirteen

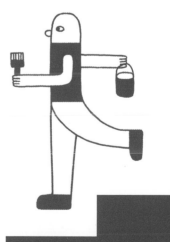

Picture Credits

front cover © Michael Moran

p. 2 © Michael Moran

p. 4 © Adam Schultz, © 2019 Sesame Workshop®, Sesame Street® and associated characters, trademarks and design elements are owned and licensed by Sesame Workshop. All rights reserved

p. 6 © Michael Moran

pp. 8–9 © James Lambert

pp. 11–13 © Michael Moran

p. 14 © Tim Schenck

p. 15 © Tim Fisher

p. 16 © Iwan Baan

pp. 17–19 © Michael Moran

p. 20 © Iwan Baan

pp. 21–27 © Michael Moran

pp. 28–29 © Jeff Goldberg

pp. 30–33 © Michael Moran

pp. 34–38 © James Lambert

p. 41 © Iwan Baan

p. 42 top © Hufton and Crow; bottom © Steve Speller

p. 43 top © Iwan Baan; bottom © Pawel Kopczynski/Reuters

p. 44 © Heatherwick Studio

p. 45 M. C. Escher, *Relativity* © 2018 The M. C. Escher Company—The Netherlands, all rights reserved, mcescher.com

pp. 46–47 © Edward Burtynsky, courtesy Nicholas Metivier Gallery, Toronto

pp. 48–57 © Heatherwick Studio

p. 58 © James Lambert

p. 59 © Related Companies

p. 60 top © James Loveday; bottom © Heatherwick Studio

p. 61 © Heatherwick Studio

p. 62 © Related Companies/Oxford

p. 63 top © Related Companies/Oxford; bottom © Joe Woolhead

pp. 64–65 © Phil O'Brien/W42ST Magazine

pp. 66–67 © Joe Woolhead

p. 68 © Ondel Hylton

pp. 69–73 © Joe Woolhead

pp. 74–79 © James Lambert

p. 82 © Skyviewsurvey.com

p. 83 © Alexander Alland, Jr./Corbis Historical via Getty Images

p. 84 © William England/Getty Images

p. 85 © ullstein bild Dtl.

p. 86 © Edwin Levick/Getty Images

pp. 88–89 © Associated Press

p. 90 © Michael Moran

p. 91 top © Timothy Fadek/Getty Images; bottom © Michael Moran

pp. 92–93 © James Lambert

p. 95 © Diane Cook and Len Jenshel/ Getty Images

pp. 98–99 © Michael Moran

pp. 100–101 © James Lambert

p. 104 top © Iwan Baan; bottom © Sebastian Kopp/EyeEm/Getty Images

p. 105 © Iwan Baan

p. 106 © Pawel Gaul/iStock

p. 107 top © andykazie/iStock; bottom © Lya Cattel/iStock

p. 108 © James Lambert

p. 109 top © Starcevic/iStock; bottom © TARDY Herv/Getty Images

p. 110 © Stock Montage/Getty Images

p. 111 © bpk/RMN—Grand Palais/ Jean-Gilles Berizzi

p. 112 © Bettmann/Getty Images

p. 113 © Iwan Baan

p. 114 © Stefano Politi Markovina/Alamy Stock Photo

p. 115 © ferrantraite/iStock

p. 117 © Library of Congress/Corbis/VCG via Getty Images

pp. 118–19 © James Lambert

p. 121 © Kyle Froman

p. 122 © Michael Moran

p. 123 © Lauren Elle

pp. 124–26 © Tim Schenck

pp. 127–28 © Jeff Goldberg

p. 129 © Michael Moran

pp. 130–31 © Iwan Baan

pp. 132–33 © Polly Brown

pp. 134–35 © Iwan Baan

p. 136 clockwise from left © Walter Haim; © Adeyinka Adegbola; © Marvin Lei; © Rex Rhee; © Annie Croll; © Yogini Patel

p. 137 clockwise from top left © Karina Scholpa Acquarone; © Florencia Aracama; © Nalisah Ali; © Related Companies/NYC Lab Middle School for Collaborative Studies; © Related Companies/NYC Lab Middle School for Collaborative Studies; © Frédéric Lère

pp. 138–39 © James Lambert

p. 141 top © Elizabeth McManus; middle © Michael Lionstar; bottom © Taylor Jewell

pp. 142–43 © Michael Moran

Author Biographies

JEFF CHU is an award-winning journalist, essayist, and author based in Princeton, New Jersey. Though he grew up mostly in California and Florida, his family hails from Hong Kong, where he gained an appreciation for unusual architecture and vertiginous skyscrapers. He previously served as a staff writer and editor at *Time* and as an editor at *Fast Company*, writing extensively about a diverse range of subjects including design, culture, international affairs, religion, and society. His work has also appeared in the *New York Times Magazine*, the *Wall Street Journal*, and *Travel + Leisure*. He is the author of the book *Does Jesus Really Love Me?* (2013).

PAUL GOLDBERGER, whom the *Huffington Post* called "the leading figure in architecture criticism," won a Pulitzer Prize for his writing in the *New York Times*. The author of several books, including *Why Architecture Matters* (2009) and *Building Art: The Life and Work of Frank Gehry* (2015), he has also served as architecture critic for the *New Yorker* and for *Vanity Fair* and holds the Joseph Urban Chair in Design and Architecture at The New School in New York City. He is currently at work on a book on the architecture of baseball parks.

SARAH MEDFORD is a journalist specializing in design and visual culture and a contributing editor at *WSJ. Magazine*, the monthly publication of the *Wall Street Journal*. A longtime magazine writer and editor, she is also author of the book *At Home with Town & Country* and has contributed essays to many other publications, including a monograph on the architect Joseph Dirand. She lives in New York City.

© Prestel Verlag, Munich · London · New York, 2019
A member of Verlagsgruppe Random House GmbH
Neumarkter Strasse 28 · 81673 Munich

Prestel Publishing Ltd.
14–17 Wells Street, London W1T 3PD

Prestel Publishing
900 Broadway, Suite 603, New York, NY 10003

Library of Congress Control Number: 2018954413

A CIP catalogue record for this book is available from
the British Library.

Editorial direction: Ali Gitlow
Copyediting: Aimee Selby
Design and layout: Studio Frith
Production management: Ann-Kathrin Koch, Imago
Separations: Dexter Premedia Ltd
Printing and binding: Shenzhen Yaleader
Digital Printing Co Ltd
Paper: Snow Eagle matte FSC®

FSC
www.fsc.org
MIX
Paper from
responsible sources
FSC® C005748

Verlagsgruppe Random House FSC® N001967

Printed in China by Imago

ISBN 978-3-7913-8473-3

www.prestel.com